KU-549-846

MARTIAL ARTS

Jillian Powell

Editorial Consultant – Cliff Moon

993064879 8

nasen
NASEN House, 4/5 Amber Business Village, Amber Close,
Amington, Tamworth, Staffordshire B77 4RP

Rising Stars UK Ltd.
22 Grafton Street, London W1S 4EX
www.risingstars-uk.com

Every effort has been made to trace copyright holders and
obtain their permission for use of copyright material. The
publisher will gladly receive information enabling them to
rectify any error or omission in subsequent editions.
All facts are correct at time of going to press.

Text © Rising Stars UK Ltd.
The right of Jillian Powell to be identified as the author of
this work has been asserted by her in accordance with the
Copyright, Design and Patents Act, 1988.

Published 2006

Cover design: Button plc
Cover image: Alamy
Illustrator: Bill Greenhead
Text design and typesetting: Marmalade Book Design
(www.marmaladebookdesign.com)
Educational consultants: Cliff Moon, Lorraine Petersen and
Paul Blum
Technical consultants: Richard Cassidy and Sean Connley
Pictures: Alamy: pages 4, 5, 7, 22, 23, 33
Empics: pages 5, 17, 24, 30, 32, 40, 41
Kobal Collection: pages 7, 17, 34, 35, 41
Stockfile: pages 6, 8, 9, 10, 11, 12, 13, 14, 15, 16, 20, 21, 26,
27, 31, 32, 42, 43

All rights reserved. No part of this publication may be
reproduced, stored in a retrieval system, or transmitted in
any form by any means, electronic, mechanical, photocopying,
recording or otherwise without the prior permission of Rising
Stars UK Ltd.

British Library Cataloguing in Publication Data.
A CIP record for this book is available from the British
Library.

ISBN: 978-1-84680-046-7

Printed by Craftprint International Ltd., Singapore

This book should not
be used as a guide to
the sports shown in it.
The publishers accept
no responsibility for
any harm which might
result from taking
part in these sports.

Contents

Fighting fit

There are many kinds of martial art.

Most martial arts began in Asia. Many people practised them as skills for fighting wars.

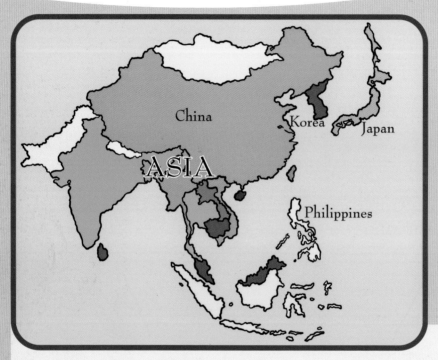

Today, people practise martial arts as sports, for **self-defence** and to keep fit.

Martial arts can give you:

- a fit body
- a fit mind
- self-confidence
- discipline
- friends.

'Martial arts' means 'War-like arts'.

There are two styles in martial arts.

Hard styles, like karate, use power and high kicks.

Soft styles use slow, flowing moves.

Most forms of t'ai chi use these kinds of moves.

Get into martial arts

Join a class.

WANT TO LEARN TAE KWON DO?

Every week, 7-9pm
Adults and children's classes
Call 1234 567890

Your library will have information on **local** martial arts classes.

See a contest or event.

Look out for **local** events or
watch contests on television.

Watch some martial arts films.

Bruce Lee, Jackie Chan and Jet Li are
famous martial arts film stars.

Martial arts classes

Students practise martial arts in a hall which is often called the dojo.

There are strict rules about:

- what to wear
- how to behave.

Each martial art is different.

But most martial arts classes follow the same kind of routine.

1 The class begins with **meditation**.

2 Then the students do warm-up exercises.

3 Students practise basic moves first.

4 Then they link the moves into patterns.

5 Finally, they practise **sparring** with a partner.

Martial arts gear

Every martial art has its own gear.

Students often wear a white suit for training.

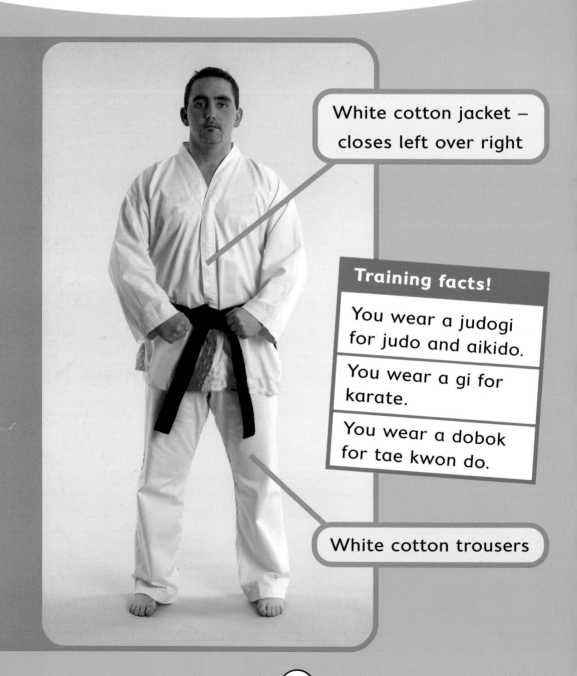

White cotton jacket – closes left over right

Training facts!

You wear a judogi for judo and aikido.

You wear a gi for karate.

You wear a dobok for tae kwon do.

White cotton trousers

Belt knotted at front

Belt facts!

The colour of the belt shows your **rank**.

Beginners in judo wear white belts.

A black belt is the highest **rank** in karate.

Safety rules

☒ Don't wear watches or jewellery

☑ Tie back long hair

☑ Keep finger- and toe-nails short

☑ Train barefoot (there are special shoes for some martial arts)

11

Ju-jitsu and aikido

Ju-jitsu began in Japan. It is one of the oldest martial arts.

'Ju-jitsu' means 'The soft art'.

Ju-jitsu uses punches, **strikes**, kicks, throws, **locks** and **grappling**!

This is a **locking** move.

Aikido came from ju-jitsu. It teaches students to fight off attacks.

'Aikido' means 'The way of harmony'.

Competitors sometimes fight with rubber knives.

Judo

Judo also came from ju-jitsu. It is one of the most popular martial arts.

In judo, two players try to wrestle or throw each other to the ground.

The players are called judoka.

There are 65 different judo throws.

This is a hip throw.

'Judo' means 'The gentle way'.

Break-falls

Judoka must learn to fall safely on the judo mat.

Tuck chin in to lift and protect the head.

Slap hands on floor to cushion force of fall.

Kung fu

Kung fu comes from China. There are lots of different styles of kung fu.

Many kung fu movements copy the fighting of animals, such as tigers, snakes and dragons.

'Kung fu' means 'work' or 'training'.

Kung fu fact!

Kung fu was first practised by monks!

Students can practise kung fu moves on a wooden dummy.

Their deadly mission: to crack the forbidden island of Han!

ENTER THE DRAGON

The ultimate Martial Arts masterpiece! Lavishly filmed by Warner Bros. in Hong Kong and the China Sea!

Bruce Lee was famous for kung fu films like **Enter the Dragon** (1973).

17

Who's the Dummy?
(Part one)

Scott's phone beeped.

It was a text from Harvey.

Come round 2nite?

Scott texted back.

Can't. Got kung fu.

Harvey sent another text.

Sounds nasty. Got a rash with it?

Scott called Harvey's number.

"Ha, ha ... . Very funny, mate. Hey, have you had any ideas for the show?"

The end-of-term summer show was next week.

"Well, we can't sing and we can't dance ..."
Harvey said.

"Wait! I've got it!" Scott said. The idea hit him
like a kung fu kick.

"We can do a kung fu display!"

"Just one small problem," Harvey said. "I can't
do kung fu."

"You can sort out the props and backdrop,"
Scott told him. "It will be great!"

Continued on page 28

19

Karate

Karate is a form of **self-defence** from Japan.

It uses kicks, **blocks** and **strikes**.

Karate kicks are high and powerful.

'Karate' means 'empty hand' because no weapons are used.

Karate **blocks** stop an **opponent**'s move.

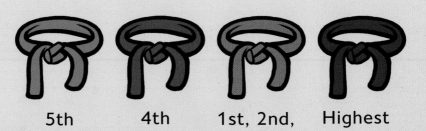

Karate **strikes** can break through wood or even bricks!

Belt ranks

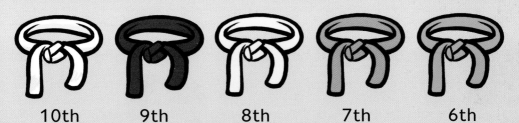

| 10th | 9th | 8th | 7th | 6th |

(or ungraded)

| 5th | 4th | 1st, 2nd, 3rd | Highest |

Kendo

Kendo began in Japan over 700 years ago. It is a kind of sword fighting.

People who practise kendo are called kendoka. They wear **protective** gear and fight with wooden or bamboo swords.

'Kendo' means 'The way of the sword'.

Kendo fact!

Kendo was used by **samurai warriors** in ancient Japan.

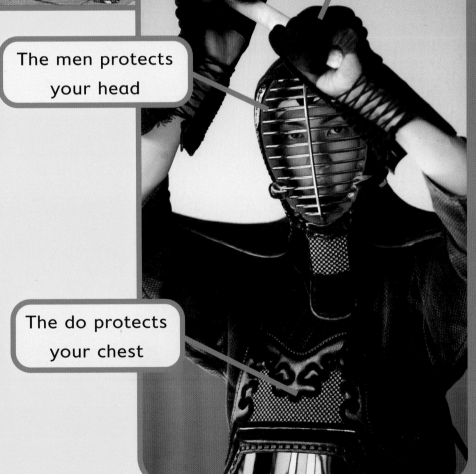

The kote are padded gloves — they protect your hands

The men protects your head

The do protects your chest

23

Sumo wrestling

Sumo is the national sport of Japan.
It is over 2,000 years old.

Sumo wrestlers are called rikishi. They fight
to push each other out of the ring.

Sumo wrestlers are big stars in Japan.

'Sumo' means 'Both rushing together'.

Sumo wrestlers live in sumo stables. They work out every day.

They eat lots of rice and **protein** foods and then sleep.

This builds their body weight.

Sumo wrestlers can weigh up to 280 kilograms.

World sumo weights	
Lightweight	under 85 kg
Middleweight	under 115 kg
Heavyweight	over 115 kg

Kick-boxing

Kick-boxers use their feet, elbows and knees as well as their fists.

Kick-boxing facts!

Thai boxing is the toughest form of kick-boxing.

It is the national sport of Thailand.

Mouth guard

Boxing gloves

Shin guards

Foot protectors

Head guards and groin protectors are also used.

Lower body moves	Upper body moves
Back kick 	**Uppercut** 
Front kick 	**Hook** 
Roundhouse kick 	**Jab** 
Knee strike 	**Right cross** 

Who's the Dummy?
(Part two)

Scott and Harvey were watching a martial arts movie.

"Hey, great move!" Harvey said. "Can you do one of those?"

"Don't be daft," Scott said. "That's wire fu. The guy is on a wire. Do you really think anyone could jump that high?"

Harvey shrugged.

Then he said, "Look, I got you a prop!"

He took a brick out of his bag.

"What do I do with that?" Scott asked him. Sometimes, Harvey did his head in!

"I thought you could chop through it, you know," Harvey chopped the air with his hand.

"Are you mad? I'd end up in hospital!" Scott said. "Look, I'll tell you what I do need – a dummy. I can use it to show **strikes** and **blocks** and stuff."

"Sorted," Harvey said.

Continued on page 36

Tae kwon do

Tae kwon do is a martial art from Korea.
There are different forms of tae kwon do.
One of the forms is an Olympic sport.

Tae kwon do fact!

Tae kwon do moves include:

- **stances**
- **blocks**
- punches
- kicks.

'Tae kwon do' means the 'The Art of Foot and Hand'.

It is famous for amazing flying kicks.

This is a jumping front kick.

T'ai chi

T'ai chi comes from China. It is a soft style of kung fu that uses slow, flowing moves.

In China, many people practise t'ai chi outdoors. They do it before or after work.

The Chinese think chi is a force within the body.

They think t'ai chi moves chi around the body and that this keeps them fit and healthy.

T'ai chi is good for:

• keeping fit

• relaxing

• **posture**

• breathing.

'T'ai chi' means 'Supreme Ultimate Fist'.

Martial arts movies

The first martial arts movies were made in Asia. The actors were martial arts **masters**.

This is from **Crouching Tiger, Hidden Dragon** (2000). The film is a story of magic, revenge and power.

Warriors fight to get back the lost sword of destiny.

Martial arts films use wire stunt work for fight sequences.

This is called wire fu. Now many films include wire stunt work.

The Matrix Reloaded (2003) has lots of wire stunt scenes.

Martial arts stars

Bruce Lee was a Chinese-American martial arts star.

He was famous for **mixed martial arts** – or **mma**.

Bruce Lee in **Enter the Dragon** (1973).

Jackie Chan films mix comedy with martial arts.

Jackie Chan in **Shanghai Knights** (2003).

Who's the Dummy?
(Part three)

Everything was set for the show.

Harvey had blown up a Bruce Lee poster for the backdrop.

It looked great!

Scott was dressed in his kung fu suit and shoes.

He had done his warm-up.

But where was Harvey?

He had the dummy!

Scott went backstage. He texted Harvey.

Where r u?

Scott's phone beeped.

On my way.

A few minutes later, Harvey arrived.

"Phew, at last!" Scott said. "Have you got the dummy?"

"Yeah, it's outside – hang on!"

Harvey disappeared. Then he came back – carrying a shop dummy!

"What's *that*?" Scott asked.

"You said 'Get a dummy'!"

"I meant a kung fu dummy – not a shop dummy!" Scott shouted. "Who's the dummy? And I'm not talking about that!"

Continued on the next page

Just then, their teacher appeared.

"You're on next," he told Scott.

"I can't go on with *that*!" Scott told Harvey.

"Wait!" said Harvey. "I've got an idea!"

Two minutes later, the music started.
They were on!

The curtain opened.

Scott did his **kung fu greeting**. Then his
opponent appeared. The audience cheered.
It was Bruce Lee! Harvey had stuck a picture of
Bruce Lee on to the dummy's face. He was
hiding at the side of the stage to move it around!

Scott did a side kick. Bruce fell over. He got up again – then Scott did an elbow **strike**. Bruce fell over again. It was fast and it was funny. Everyone loved it!

"Who's the dummy now?" asked Harvey.

Capoeira

Capoeira comes from Brazil. African slaves invented it as a form of **self-defence**.

Many capoeira moves are based on African dance.

They include sweeps, kicks and headbutts.

Capoeira music, songs and clapping go along with the moves.

'Capoeira' means 'Wheel, ring or chicken coop'.

You can see capoeira in these computer and video games:

- Tekken 3, 4 and 5

- Street Fighter III

- Fatal Fury

You can see capoeira in these films:

- **Meet the Fockers** (2004)

- **Ocean's Twelve** (2004)

- **Catwoman** (2004).

Capoeira facts!

Capoeira uses coloured cords to show **ranks**.

They are the same colours as the Brazilian flag.

More martial arts

Eskrima

Eskrima comes from the Philippines.

It is stick or sword fighting.

It began as a way of defending tribes against attack.

The eskrima sword is called a kali.

Hapkido

Hapkido is a form of **self-defence** from Korea.

It uses **grappling**, striking and kicking moves.

Savate

Savate is French kick-boxing. It began as a type of street-fighting.

Boxers use their hands and feet as weapons.

Martial arts fact!

Weapons are also used in some Indian martial arts.

Quiz

1 What is a dojo?

2 What is a gi?

3 Which colour belt do judo beginners wear?

4 Which colour belt do masters of karate wear?

5 What does 'ju-jitsu' mean?

6 Which martial art's name means 'empty hand'?

7 Which martial art is the national sport of Japan?

8 From which country does t'ai chi come?

9 What is wire fu?

10 What is savate?

Glossary of terms

block	move to stop an opponent's attack.
break-fall	way of falling that protects you from being hurt.
dobok	training uniform for tae kwon do.
grappling	clutching or gripping move where bodies are in contact.
kung fu greeting	formal way of greeting an opponent before kung fu.
local	near to your home.
lock	hold that stops an opponent from moving.
masters	highly skilled experts.
meditation	way of calming the mind.
mixed martial arts	a sport that mixes different martial arts.
opponent	person who fights against another in a martial art or other sport.
posture	the way you stand and move.
protective	stops you being hurt.
protein	found in foods like meat, fish, cheese and nuts.
rank	level or grade of skills.
samurai warriors	sword fighters who lived in Japan long ago.
self-defence	art of defending against attack.
sparring	contest between partners.
stance	formal pose – you often do them to prepare for a move.
strike	blow to an opponent's body.

More resources

Books

Martial Arts (Super Guides) by David Mitchell
Published by Dorling Kindersley
ISBN: 0751328154

Martial Arts by Bernie Blackall
Published by Heinemann Library
ISBN: 0431036578

Magazines

Combat (Paragon Martial Arts Magazines)

Martial Arts Illustrated (Paragon Martial Arts Magazines)

Websites

http://.library.thinkquest.org/C0112643/
M[art]2-ial is a multimedia website packed with interactive
information, music and video clips.

www.ukmao.co.uk
Website featuring martial arts equipment, with links to clubs,
and a forum and message board on martial arts.

www.phonixtkd.com
Website which gives information on training for tae kwon do.

DVDs

**VMA Series – The Complete Guide to the World of Martial
Arts** (2005)
Summersdale Productions (Cat. No. B000BNT9EO)
Demonstrations of many different martial arts, including thai
boxing and t'ai chi.

Dragon – The Bruce Lee Story (1993)
Universal Pictures (Cat. No. B00004I9P7)
Movie about the life of Bruce Lee.

Answers

1 A hall where martial arts competitions and practices are held.

2 A white suit worn for karate and other martial arts.

3 White belt

4 Black belt

5 The soft art

6 Karate

7 Sumo wrestling

8 China

9 Wire stunt work in martial arts movies.

10 French kick-boxing

Special thanks to: Alexander Booth, Hannah Bush, Elizabeth Dodd, James Emblin, Angel Pooley and Alex Richardson.

Index